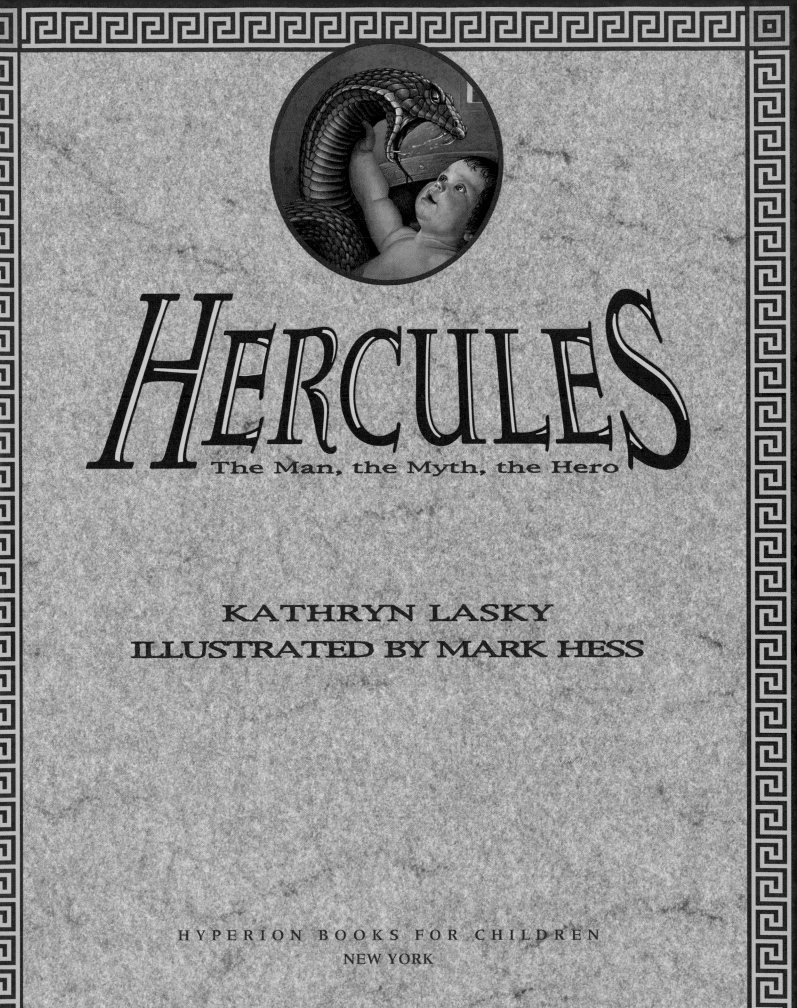

HERCULES
The Man, the Myth, the Hero

KATHRYN LASKY

ILLUSTRATED BY MARK HESS

HYPERION BOOKS FOR CHILDREN
NEW YORK

*L*isten to my tale, one of cunning and glory. A story of a monster and a man, a hero and a man. But all with one name: Hercules. It is *my* story.

Once long ago I was not called Hercules but Palaemon. Although my mother was mortal, my father was the mightiest of all the gods, Zeus: king of Olympus. His queen was Hera. But Zeus often took other wives, mortal ones who gave him children. This poisoned Hera with jealousy.

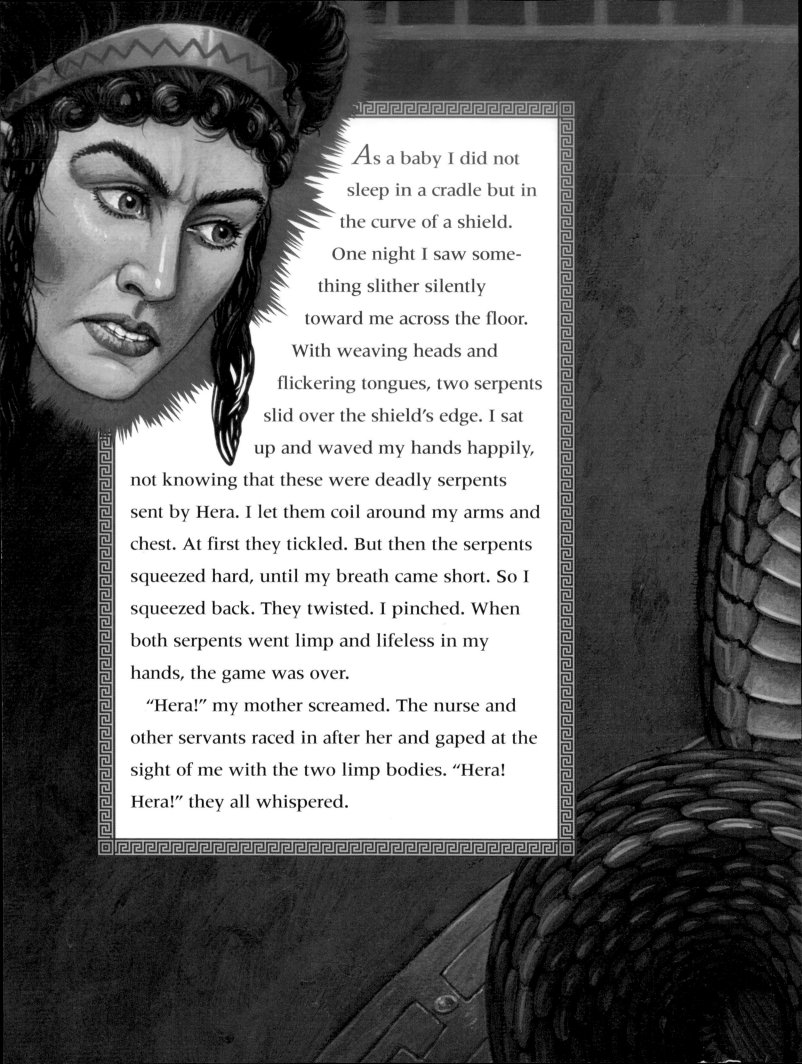

*A*s a baby I did not sleep in a cradle but in the curve of a shield. One night I saw something slither silently toward me across the floor. With weaving heads and flickering tongues, two serpents slid over the shield's edge. I sat up and waved my hands happily, not knowing that these were deadly serpents sent by Hera. I let them coil around my arms and chest. At first they tickled. But then the serpents squeezed hard, until my breath came short. So I squeezed back. They twisted. I pinched. When both serpents went limp and lifeless in my hands, the game was over.

"Hera!" my mother screamed. The nurse and other servants raced in after her and gaped at the sight of me with the two limp bodies. "Hera! Hera!" they all whispered.

*F*or many years Hera left us in peace. I learned boxing and archery, astronomy and philosophy, fencing and riding. Music too—how to sing and play the lyre. I did not learn the awesome power of my strength, however, until one day when my music teacher made me do the scales again and again. Becoming impatient, I hit him with my lyre. The man crumpled. My teacher was dead!

"I didn't mean to kill him. I really didn't," I cried to my mother. She looked at me as if I were not her son but some terrible monster. I felt hot with shame.

That was when I began to understand that I was neither quite a man nor a god. What was I? Perhaps what my mother saw—a monster. I was sent away.

"Go, Palaemon," she said. "Go to where there are wild animals to kill and not teachers." I was sent to the rugged mountain country.

*S*oon I had rid the countryside of lions and wolves. The farmers offered me gifts of food and wine and beds in their small homes. They even offered me their daughters in marriage. But I preferred to sleep under the stars. As for a wife, it seemed impossible. Ever since I had accidentally killed my music teacher, I was frightened to be around people. My own strength scared me except when I fought a ferocious animal. There were, however, other enemies besides wild animals.

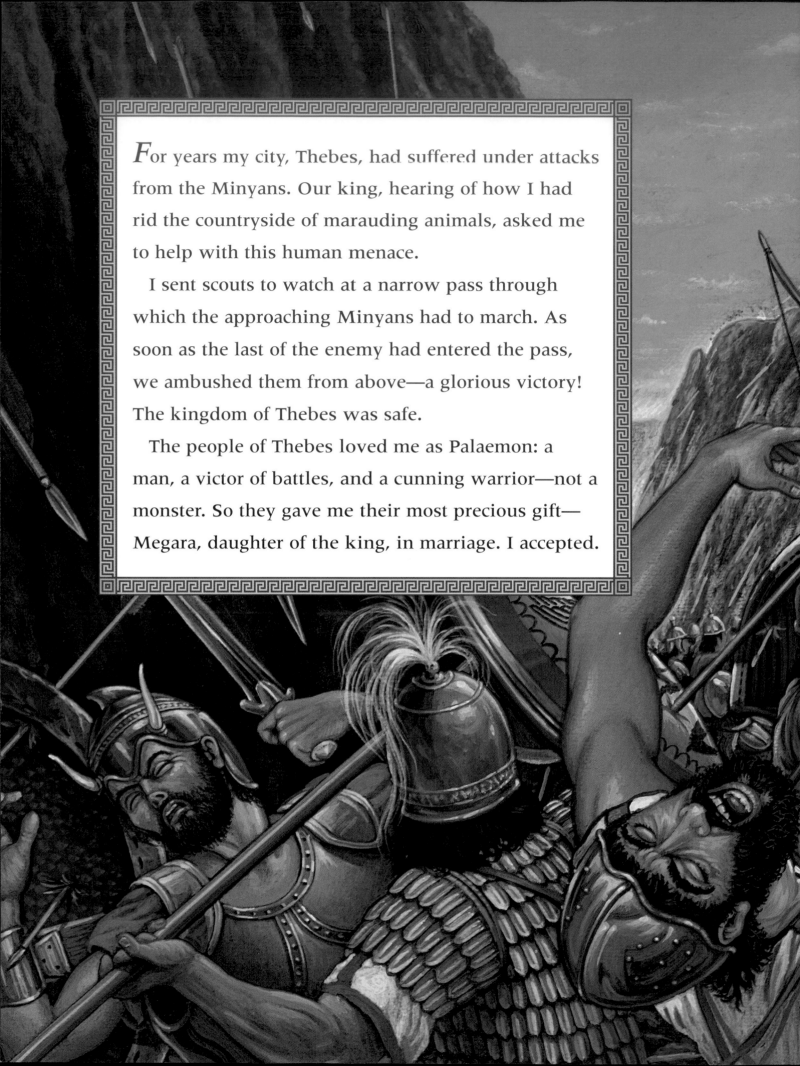

For years my city, Thebes, had suffered under attacks from the Minyans. Our king, hearing of how I had rid the countryside of marauding animals, asked me to help with this human menace.

I sent scouts to watch at a narrow pass through which the approaching Minyans had to march. As soon as the last of the enemy had entered the pass, we ambushed them from above—a glorious victory! The kingdom of Thebes was safe.

The people of Thebes loved me as Palaemon: a man, a victor of battles, and a cunning warrior—not a monster. So they gave me their most precious gift— Megara, daughter of the king, in marriage. I accepted.

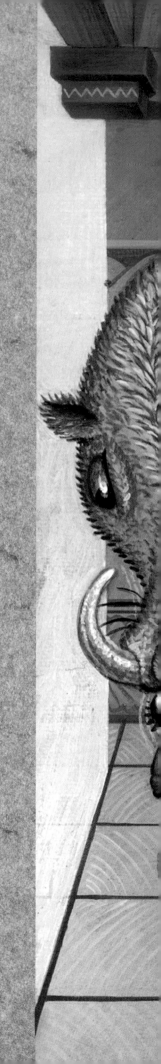

We married, had children, and were very happy. I never thought of Hera. It was as if she had vanished.

One afternoon in the courtyard I felt a shadow slide across my mind. Then a deep despair. From the window of the nursery of my children came a terrible hissing, an echo of the two serpents that Hera had sent when I was a baby. I raced inside. I could not see my children, nor two serpents, but at least ten! And wild boars and a lion, its fangs dripping blood. I drew my sword and lunged and slashed until nothing moved. My children were safe.

I blinked, and the shadow and despair slipped away. Beasts did not lie at my feet but my own wife and children. And another voice from a distant time echoed and then pounded in my head. "Hera! Hera!" This time Hera had not sent serpents but madness. I was drowning in my horror and shame.

*T*he people had been wrong: I was a monster! I went to a sacred place, the shrine of Apollo at Delphi, to ask the oracle how I could ever purify myself and be forgiven.

"You shall no longer be called Palaemon," the priestess said. "You are from this moment forth *Hercules*, 'Hera's glory,' since it is from Hera that you shall have everlasting fame. Now, go to Tiryns and serve your cousin King Eurystheus, performing the twelve labors he asks of you. If you successfully do his bidding, you shall be forgiven."

I had no choice and set forth.

"You are to kill the terrible lion of Nemea who preys on people and the flocks of farmers," demanded Eurystheus upon my arrival. He paused as if listening to a voice only he could hear. I realized that Hera, though invisible, was present. "Not just kill," he continued, "but flay the lion." This had to be Hera's idea, for the beast had a skin like stone.

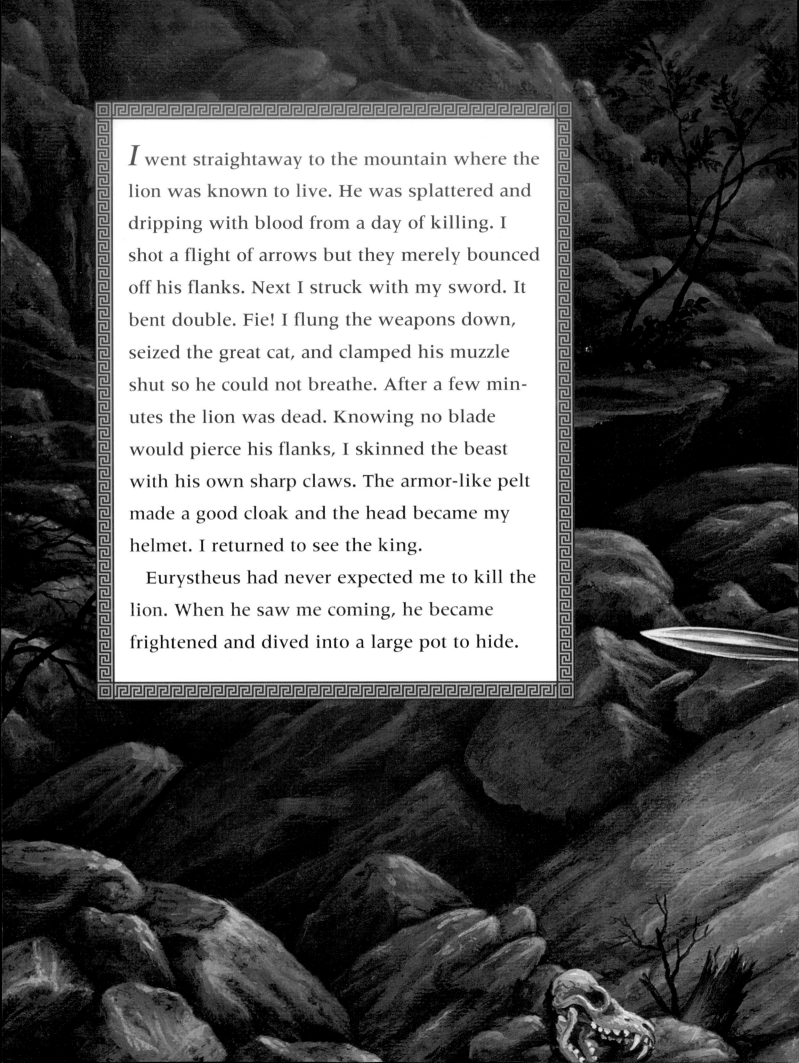

I went straightaway to the mountain where the lion was known to live. He was splattered and dripping with blood from a day of killing. I shot a flight of arrows but they merely bounced off his flanks. Next I struck with my sword. It bent double. Fie! I flung the weapons down, seized the great cat, and clamped his muzzle shut so he could not breathe. After a few minutes the lion was dead. Knowing no blade would pierce his flanks, I skinned the beast with his own sharp claws. The armor-like pelt made a good cloak and the head became my helmet. I returned to see the king.

Eurystheus had never expected me to kill the lion. When he saw me coming, he became frightened and dived into a large pot to hide.

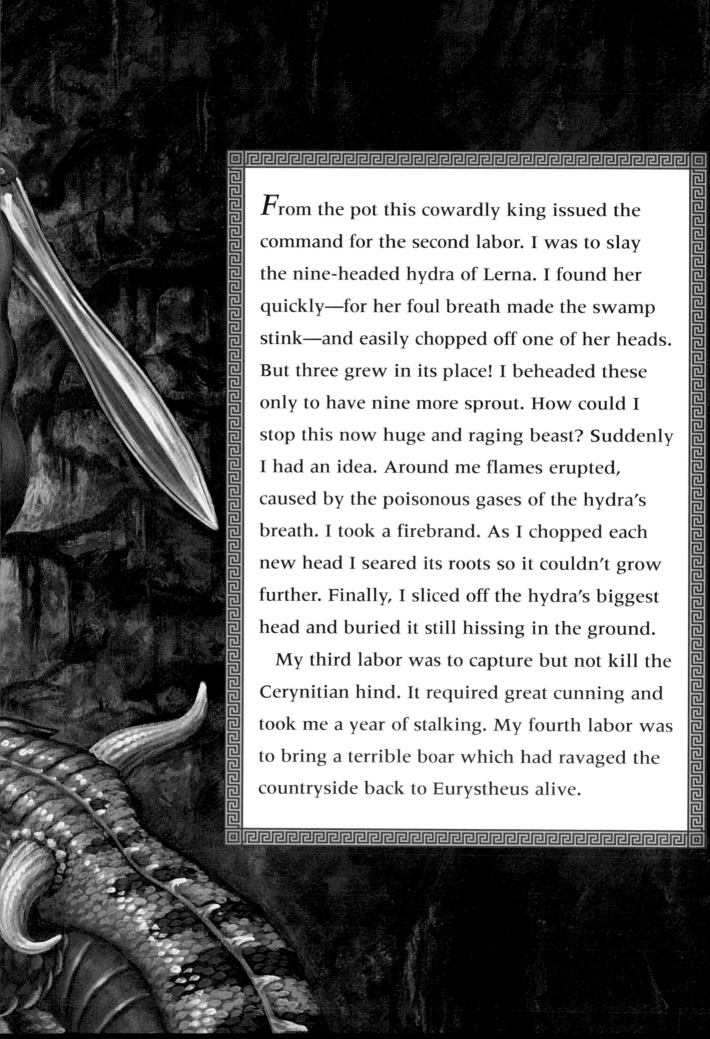

From the pot this cowardly king issued the command for the second labor. I was to slay the nine-headed hydra of Lerna. I found her quickly—for her foul breath made the swamp stink—and easily chopped off one of her heads. But three grew in its place! I beheaded these only to have nine more sprout. How could I stop this now huge and raging beast? Suddenly I had an idea. Around me flames erupted, caused by the poisonous gases of the hydra's breath. I took a firebrand. As I chopped each new head I seared its roots so it couldn't grow further. Finally, I sliced off the hydra's biggest head and buried it still hissing in the ground.

My third labor was to capture but not kill the Cerynitian hind. It required great cunning and took me a year of stalking. My fourth labor was to bring a terrible boar which had ravaged the countryside back to Eurystheus alive.

"*Y*ou failed!" Eurystheus shrieked when I returned with my hands and clothes spotless from my fifth labor. With Hera's help, he had devised what they believed to be an impossible and shameful task. I was to clean out the filthy stables of King Augeas, where dung was piled high as mountains.

"The stables are clean," I answered. "By moving huge boulders I changed the course of two rivers so the water swept through the stables and washed the filth away."

For the sixth labor I had to destroy a flock of flesh-eating birds. For the seventh, I captured the bull of Crete.

I stole the horses of King Diomedes for the eighth labor, and for the ninth I brought back the golden girdle of the Amazon queen. Then I sailed far to seize the cattle of a monster named Geryon.

*F*or the eleventh labor I traveled west. There, guarded by a horrible dragon was Hera's tree that bore golden apples. I killed the dragon, but was wary to pluck the fruit myself, as Eurystheus had ordered. Seeing Atlas nearby gave me an idea.

"You look weary, my friend. I shall hold the sky for you, if you fetch Hera's golden apples from her garden."

"Here are your apples," Atlas said, returning in a short time. "But let me take them to Eurystheus for you."

He doesn't wish to take back the burden of the sky, I thought. "All right," I said. "Just hold the sky a moment while I make a pad of my lion skin to ease the weight." Atlas was tricked, and I ran off with the apples.

The final labor was to fetch Cerberus, the three-headed monster dog, from Hades.

My labors were finished, my earlier shame and horror put to rest. My glory complete. But my story was not over.

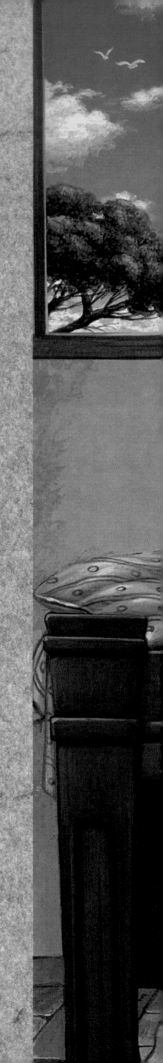

Shortly afterward I visited an old friend. All through dinner I felt another presence in the room. My host—a quiet, peaceful man—suddenly jumped up and falsely accused me of stealing his horses. I grew incensed. Just before I saw her shadow, the shadow of Hera, my anger exploded. I struck out at my host, but his son stood between us. I was sorry before the boy's body hit the ground but it was too late. I then heard her terrible laughter. "Hera!" I screamed. "Fie on you! You are my shame."

Once more I went to the oracle at Delphi. "You have murdered the son of your host!" she cried. "*Slave* you shall now be called—slave for Queen Omphale of Lydia, and you shall wear a dress instead of your lion's pelt and a woman's turban instead of a helmet, and you shall spin and embroider. And by this you shall tame the monster within you." The shame stung me like the bite of a thousand wasps. And in the distant clouds I heard not a rumble of thunder but the laughter of Hera.

I served Queen Omphale obediently. When my service was done I put on my pelt and helmet again. I prayed that the monster within me slept, and I prayed that I might find a new wife. I did. Her name was Deianira.

One day Deianira and I came to a river in full flood. I saw a centaur frolicking in the shallows and in the glinting light I thought for a moment he swam with a woman. My breath locked. Was it Hera? But it must have been the play of the light on the water, for the centaur, named Nessus, rose out of the river quite alone and offered to carry Deianira across.

Once on the other side, however, he tried to run off with her. Taking careful aim I shot an arrow. The centaur dropped and blood poured from his wound. I saw him whisper something to my wife. I thought nothing of it until many years later. . . .

I returned home last night after several weeks away. Deianira seemed different to me; she acted suspiciously. She brought me a shirt she had woven herself with rusty streaks in it. "A gift for my husband," she said. Pleased, I put it on. Immediately the cloth began to chafe my skin, burning worse with each passing second.

"What have you done?" I cried.

"Forgive me!" she wailed. "It is stained with the blood of the centaur from long years ago. He said it would make you faithful to me always. I heard you loved another. It was a trick."

I remembered Nessus and the fleeting figure of a woman that I thought was mere light on water. Hera. Hera again. Invisible flames flared within me. I had never known such pain. And yet I felt no rage. For the first time I did not want to strike out. Hera could not rouse my anger.

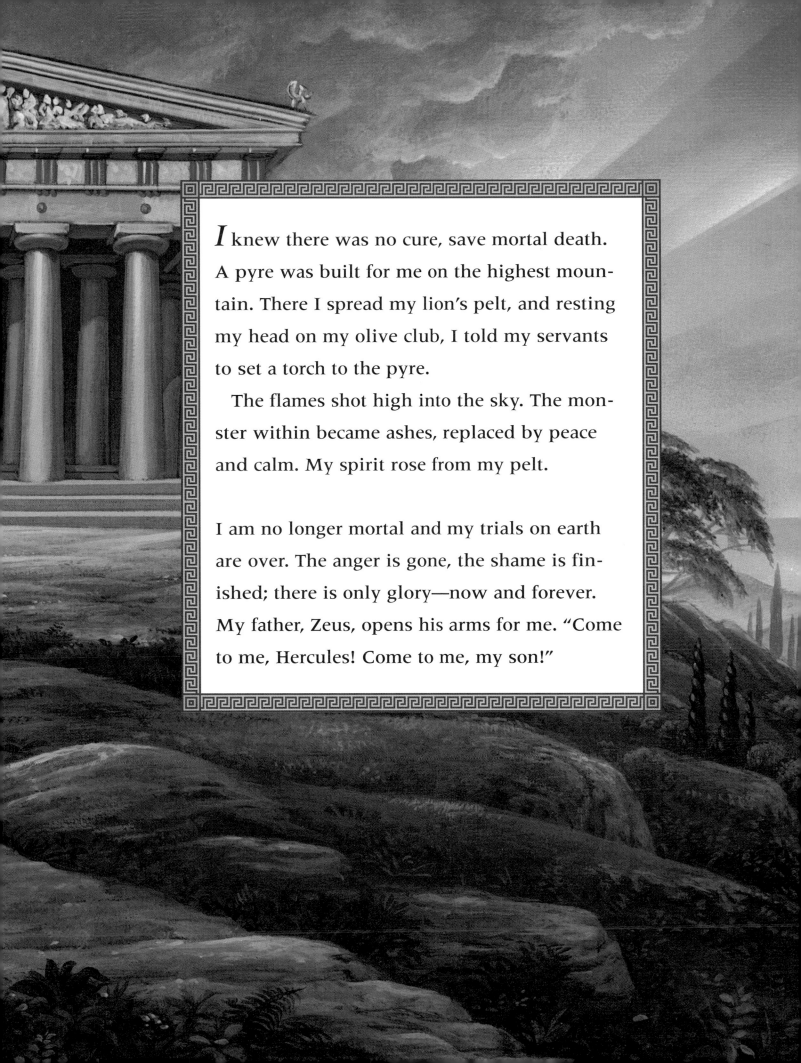

I knew there was no cure, save mortal death. A pyre was built for me on the highest mountain. There I spread my lion's pelt, and resting my head on my olive club, I told my servants to set a torch to the pyre.

The flames shot high into the sky. The monster within became ashes, replaced by peace and calm. My spirit rose from my pelt.

I am no longer mortal and my trials on earth are over. The anger is gone, the shame is finished; there is only glory—now and forever. My father, Zeus, opens his arms for me. "Come to me, Hercules! Come to me, my son!"

To my favorite heroes: Rachel, Alec, and Elyssa
—M. H.

AUTHOR'S NOTE

*H*ercules was the first superhero. The message of the superhero is a compelling one for children as well as adults: through toiling and suffering, people can overcome evil. Or, as one classicist wrote of Hercules, "Born a man—risen to god; suffered toils—conquered heaven."

In ancient Greece as well as through the centuries, there have been dozens of different tellings of Hercules' story. Mythographers have over the years chosen to emphasize some aspects while ignoring others. Depending on when the story was told, various historical events might be reflected in the telling. Which is the right one? In general, classicists do not believe that there is one authentic version of the myth. The timelessness that we associate with myths and the intrinsic flexibility of their narrative structure defy limiting these stories in such a manner.

Classicist Walter Burkert has said that myth is a traditional tale with a reference to something of collective importance. I decided that this would be my standard. I would retell the story in a manner that would have the best chance of having a "collective importance" for a wide range of young children today, but would not lose the story elements that make Hercules great. In this way I felt I could be most faithful to what I perceive as the spirit of mythology in general and the Hercules myth in particular.

Hercules' glory is that he not only vanquishes the beasts and monsters he encounters but also conquers his passions (incited by Hera) and is thus elevated to godlike stature. I had to balance the extreme violence, a common thread of all the versions I read, with the sensibilities of the young readership and my responsibility to them as an author. I did not want an inappropriate tale, but I did want a story that like all the greatest myths tells a truth, even though it is pure fiction in its most extreme, fantastic, and extraordinary form.

Among the books I found helpful in researching this book are: *Structure and History in Greek Mythology and Ritual* (Univ. of Calif. Press), by Walter Burkert; *The Greek Myths*, complete edition (Penguin), by Robert Graves; *The Nature of Greek Myths* (Penguin), by G. S. Kirk; *Myths of Greece and Rome* (Penguin), by Thomas Bulfinch; and *Mythology, Timeless Tales of Gods and Heroes* (Penguin), by Edith Hamilton.

ARTIST'S NOTE

I began my research by relying on an old and trusted friend: the local library. I then broadened my search to include museums, larger library collections, and special bookstores. I reviewed hundreds of depictions of Hercules rendered by countless artists over the centuries. I also solicited the opinions of experts in the field of Greek studies to help me decide certain details (especially lucid was the advice of Jane Mertens, curator of the Greek and Roman Department at the Metropolitan Museum of Art in New York City). I photographed Greek statuary as well as friends, family, and bodybuilders draped with makeshift costumes.

There is no authentic version of Hercules—no single tale. So, too, my art is a deliberate mixture of styles and periods. It is familiar, yet new.

Text © 1997 by Kathryn Lasky.• Illustrations © 1997 by Mark Hess. • All rights reserved. No part of this book may be reproduced or transmitted in any form or by any means, electronic or mechanical, including photocopying, recording, or by any information storage and retrieval system, without written permission from the publisher. For information address Hyperion Books for Children, 114 Fifth Avenue, New York, New York, 10011-5690.• Printed in the United States of America.• First Edition • 1 3 5 7 9 10 8 6 4 2 • The artwork for each picture is prepared using acrylic on canvas.• This book is set in 14-point Meridien Medium.• Library of Congress Cataloging-in-Publication Data • Lasky, Kathryn Hercules: the man, the myth, the hero/Kathyn Lasky; illustrated by Mark Hess. — 1st ed.• p. cm. • Includes bibliographical references. • Summary: Recounts the story of the mythological hero, Hercules, child of Zeus and a mortal woman, including his twelve labors and ending with his ascension to Mount Olympus as a god.• ISBN 0-7868-0329-0 (trade)—ISBN 0-7868-2274-0 (lib. bdg.) • 1. Heracles (Greek mythology)—Juvenile literature. [1. Heracles (Greek mythology) 2. Mythology, Greek.] I. Hess, Mark, ill. II. Title.• BL820.H5L37 1997 • 292.2'113—dc21